SOME SHORTISH HOMILIES
for the Sundays in Ordinary Time
Year B

G000042161

GLORIFYING
THE LORD
BY YOUR LIFE

James O'Kane

Acknowledgment

Use has been made throughout of the English version of Volume I of the Roman Lectionary approved for use in Ireland in 1981.

The Homilist

Father James O'Kane was born in Belfast where he received his earliest education from Dominican Sisters and at Christian Brothers' schools. After seminary formation in Belfast and Rome he undertook postgraduate studies at Louvain and was ordained in 1976. From 1979 he taught spiritual and moral theology at Maynooth. Since 1995 he has served in Newtownards & Comber, Ballintoy & Ballinlea, Culfeightrin, Kilcoo and Cushendun & Torr.

Second Sunday

*Speak, Lord, your servant is
listening.*

Vocation, brothers and sisters in
Christ, is a religious concept. The
idea is that God calls each one of us
by name and that the meaning of our
lives is to be found in the generosity
of our response to that call. This is
not at all the way the world sees
human life. The world speaks to us
of ambition, achievement, self-
affirmation. To listen to the voice of
the world is to become entangled in
the endless pursuit of material
security and satisfaction - an absorb-
ing pursuit whose pointlessness is
not immediately obvious. Vocation is
a radically different approach, an
approach that is incompatible with
the ways of the world.

Vocation is about being called by God. Today's gospel tells us about the straightforward way some of the first disciples were called. Jesus is pointed out to them. They recognize him as the Messiah. And their lives are never the same again. Vocation implies conversion: leaving the past behind and moving on in a surprisingly different direction.

The vocation of each one of us is personal and unique. God calls each one of us by his or her own name just as he called the young Samuel. Samuel heard his name but he did not know that it was God who was calling him until the fourth time when with Eli's help he was ready with the right response: Speak, Lord, your servant is listening.

Few of us get the start in life that Samuel had. His parents offered him to the Lord from his earliest childhood. They did not launch him into life burdened with their own pathetic disappointments and foolish aspirations. When the time came he had the freedom to respond in the right way: Speak, Lord, your servant is listening. It is not something that we find easy to say. We have our own agenda, our own plans, our own projects. We are burdened by original sin, handed on with a strange fidelity from one generation to the next. We have even prayed for success. We have begged God to do it our way. Our vocation does not even begin until such prayer is silenced - and replaced by this radically new form of prayer: Speak, Lord, your servant is listening.

And there lies all the difference between Christian prayer and pagan prayer. The pagan uses many words and makes a long speech. His aim is to make things clear to God. The disciple of Jesus uses few and familiar words: Thy Kingdom come. Thy will be done. He knows that he is called above all to listen. And when he has heard the voice of God his prayer imitates the prayer of Jesus himself: Not my will but thine. Here I am, Lord, I come to do your will. The prayer of the true disciple is the prayer of Mary and of all the saints: Be it done unto me according to thy word. Like every true disciple of Jesus before us we are constantly being called to leave our past behind and to move on, into the challenge, and holy freedom, of what is yet to come.

First Samuel 3:3-10. 19 / First Corinthians 6:13-15. 17-20 / John 1:35-42

Third Sunday

The time has come. The kingdom of God is close at hand. Repent and believe the Good News.

Today's gospel, brothers and sisters in Christ, tells us of the beginnings of Our Lord's preaching activity and the calling of his first apostles: the brothers Simon and Andrew and the sons of Zebedee, James and John. To these fishermen he says abruptly: Follow me and I will make you into fishers of men.

Repent and believe the Good News. Come follow me. Two dimensions of the same call - addressed just as personally to us as it was to those first apostles. Repent and believe the Good News. Come follow me. This call to repentance and discipleship never loses anything of its freshness and relevance. We are always at the beginning of our conversion. We are always in need of a deeper con-version. Every day the Lord calls us anew. He calls us to change, to leave a little more of our sinfulness behind. He calls us to follow him along the road of truth and freedom and love that will lead us through the cross to resurrection.

There have been dramatic conversions and very public conversions. We think of Saint Paul and Saint Augustine: Paul relieved of his anti-Christian rage on the road to Damascus, Augustine rescued once and for all from his self-indulgence while reading some verses of Paul's letter to the Romans. But for most us conversion takes place a little at a time, from day to day, a gentle increase in the generosity and fidelity of our response to the demands of the Good News of Jesus Christ.

Still, this way of seeing our conversion as the work of a lifetime removes nothing of its urgency, for, as Paul today reminds us: Our time is growing short. The world as we know it is passing away. Of course the business of life is important but it has in the end only a relative importance. We are to make the best use of what the world has to offer but without being enslaved by it. We are to be committed to the world we live in but in a distinctively detached way that allows us to leave everything when the Master calls us to move on to something else.

The world as we know it is passing away. Repent and believe the Good News. We are invited to grow in freedom, to develop a greater detach-ment. Those who know this freedom and this detachment are in fact strengthened in their commitment to everyday life. They are no longer afraid of a new and unexpected call to leave everything and follow Christ more closely. They know that such a call can come at any time and that they will be ready for it when it does.

And so this work of a lifetime that is also a daily challenge is to be taken seriously. If we put off our con-version until tomorrow we risk being lost. On the last day tomorrow's conversion will count for nothing. It is what we allow life to make of us today that decides our eternal destiny.

We notice that in Nineveh Jonah had no need of a long sermon. Only forty days more and Nineveh is going to be destroyed. Brief and to the point and, in the case of Nineveh, singularly effective. Each one of us in our own heart knows quite well what conversion would imply for us. The preacher has only to recall the words of Jesus: The time has come. The kingdom of God is at hand. Repent and believe the Good News. And, if only we will allow it, the grace of God will do the rest.

Jonah 3:1-5. 10 / First Corinthians 7:29-31 / Mark 1:14-20

Fourth Sunday

The people were so astonished that they started asking each other what it all meant.

Authority, and astonishment, and quietness. Three things, brothers and sisters in Christ, we cannot always count on when we come to Sunday Mass. Jesus teaches with authority. He tells evil spirits to be quiet. And people are so astonished that they start asking each other what it all means. Jesus is of course the envy of every preacher. We would all like to astonish our audience into asking themselves what it all means. But somehow like the scribes in Jesus' day we don't seem to teach with any real authority.

What we have to say makes little or no impression. If people do go home talking about something we've said it's probably for all the wrong reasons. Unlike the scribes, Jesus taught with authority. People could sense that he knew what he was talking about. What he said rang true and when he spoke his words had immediate effect. They made things happen.

I do not know whether or not the scribes were able to drive out evil spirits but I suspect that their exorcisms involved a good deal of huffing and puffing and prancing about. Jesus has just to say 'Be quiet' and that's it. They're gone. He would like to exorcise our evil spirits too - but of course there's nothing to exorcise, is there? There's nothing like that wrong with us. We are in our right mind. We know exactly who we are and what we want - only too well.

But I wonder is that really true? When we are offered moments of silence in the Mass, for example, to allow us to become present to ourself in the presence of God, do you never notice just how difficult that is, to be present to yourself, to be calm and quiet and together in the silence of prayer, truly aware of who you are and who you are called to be? Or at the end of the Mass when you are sent back to your world outside, encouraged to go there in peace, glorifying the Lord by your life, is there any little seed planted at all that survives the instant forgetfulness that hits you as you make for the door?

You see, our heads are full of distractions of every kind and our hearts are bursting with the strangest longings. And yet we deny that we are possessed. Even when we do try to pray there is such a commotion going on inside us, the same old recordings playing on relentlessly the same old sad stories churning up all the same old emotions. We never hear Jesus whispering to us to be quiet, to be calm, to be still, to allow God his chance. For God does want to free us from our demons, and what astonishment there would be around us if only we would let him. In the meantime, it would be no harm if we were to start asking each other what it all means, for it is in such asking that answers begin to emerge.

Deuteronomy 18:15-20 / First Corinthians 7:32-35 / Mark 1:21-28

11

Fifth Sunday

And the fever left her and she began to wait on them.

It should not surprise us, brothers and sisters in Christ, that Simon's mother-in-law has taken to her bed, when we know the background. The news has reached her that Simon and Andrew have left their fishing-nets and gone off after this strange preacher from Nazareth. She is nearly out of her mind with worry for her daughter and the children. What will they all do, how will they survive at all, with Simon not working any more? And now she hears that they were all coming to the house looking to be fed. This is really the last straw. No wonder that she is laid low with fever.

Jesus is told about her straightaway. It sounds more like an apology than a prayer. But no doubt Simon is hoping that Jesus will make things right between him and his mother-in-law. And so it is that he goes in to her, takes her by the hand and helps her up. And that's the end of it. The fever leaves her, and she begins to wait on them.

And so it is that Simon's mother-in-law gets her explanation of what Jesus is about. No words, no long sermon, but instead the lived experience of her own trans-formation. We are all called in the same way - out of the fever we have made of our lives, into the freedom of serving the community of believers to which we now belong. No words can explain this freedom to the outsider. The most the world can offer us is a cheap freedom to do as we please. Jesus offers us the freedom to do what is right, and to do what is right, not like Job's slave sighing for the shade, not like his workman with no thought but his wages, but with the Christian joy of knowing that the Holy Spirit of God has freed us at last from all the fevers and frustrations of our own self-concern, the long night that knows no dawn, the long day of impatience and paralysis.

How does it happen, this miracle of freedom? How does paralysing self-concern become joyful service of others? Simon's mother-in-law could have locked her doors and refused to see him. We know plenty of people who adopt that strategy.* It is, after all, most often easier to accept present discomfort than face the pain of change. We need to let Jesus into our lives. We need to let him look upon our trouble with his eyes of love. We need to let him take us by the hand and help us up. This is resurrection and it is in our surrender to it that our miracle happens. We are set free from the fevers that have possessed us and begin to know the joys of service.

Job 7:1-4. 6-7 / First Corinthians 9:16-19. 22-23 / Mark 1:29-39

Sixth Sunday

A leper came to Jesus and pleaded on his knees: If you want to, he said, you can cure me.

Leprosy, brothers and sisters in Christ, is a powerful symbol of all those things that exclude us from the richness of ordinary life. The loathsome physical symptoms are by no means the most distressing aspect of this disease. It is the exclusion from our everyday togetherness that is so painful and shocking. For we forget, and the leper is urged to forget, that before sickness struck they were ordinary people just like the rest of us.

And so, uncomfortably, we are reminded of our attitude to lepers of whatever kind, all those people we are inclined to treat as such. We are reminded too of any leprosy of our own that excludes us, in whatever way, from being fully part of the life going on around us. And we are reminded of the compassion of Jesus and how we are called to receive it in our own person and imitate it in our lives. Jesus stretched out his hand and touched him. We too may hope to be touched by divine mercy and so find ourselves enabled to reach out and touch those we see marginalized and excluded in our own environment.

What perhaps surprises us is the stern way Jesus orders this man who has been cured of his leprosy to go away and say nothing to anyone. This is less surprising, though, when we consider the consequences of the man's betrayal. He started talking about it freely and telling the story everywhere - so that Jesus could no longer go openly into any town, but had to stay outside in places where nobody lived. Because of his compassion, Jesus himself is made a kind of leper, no longer able to reach out and heal the pain of others. Such indeed is often the cost of compassion.

And somehow religion is undermined by gossip about miracles, and faith squandered - for we like the idea of easy miracles. It is an old temptation. The message of Jesus is that only the truth will set us free. Miracles happen when we accept our truth. But they are our miracles, God's kindness to us, an expression of his compassion. We owe him our silence. We undermine God's work when we promise others easy miracles, without commitment. We forget the price of miracles. If you want to, the leper said, you can cure me. But as he stretched out his hand to touch the leper, Jesus cannot have known with certainty what would happen. Such is the risk of compassion. For it is in the uncertainty of faith that we find all the difference between dictating to God what he must do to keep us happy and graciously accepting the miracles that flow from trusting him in all things and accepting his will.

We too will find our healing on our knees before Jesus. If you want to, Lord, you can cure me. There we will find our personal truth and our healing, as much miracle as we need. Jesus will forever elude us if we waste our lives pursuing the mirage of other people's miracles. We are to await our own in the stillness and truth of our prayer.

Leviticus 13:1-2. 44-46 / First Corinthians 10:31 – 11:1 / Mark 1:40-45

Seventh Sunday

They were all astounded and praised God saying, We have never seen anything like this.

There is, brothers and sisters in Christ, a certain kind of astounding sympathy that forgives and heals, and reminds us that much that is wrong with us could be healed were we ever enabled to know forgiveness and forgive ourselves. Only God, we say, can forgive sin, that great wound that separates us from ourselves and from others. And so it must be that God is indeed present at the core of this sympathy that heals such wounds and makes us whole again.

Sin is, of course, a kind of paralysis. The sinner, for all his frenetic activity, is trapped inside his own little world of self-concern. Forgiveness enables him to break out, to get up and go home, and to be at home where he really belongs. To have made a really good confession, even once in our life, is to remember that experience forever, and to hope that it can be repeated, that our moment of grace will come again.

My child, Jesus said, your sins are forgiven. Some say that it is the child in us that needs healing, for it is in childhood that the seeds of sin are sown. The child's traumas are the roots of later anxieties. It is the wounded child in us that is paralysed when faced with the responsibilities of our adult years. If we cannot do what is right as adults it is often because we have been taught as children to fear doing what is wrong. We are paralysed by that fear.

Jesus does not wait for the man to confess anything. He addresses the child instead: My child, your sins are forgiven. Forgiveness is freedom, freedom at last to be ourselves and to act freely in the adult world. I order you, Jesus says to the man, get up, pick up your stretcher, and go off home. If we ourselves go to confession it must be that we somehow hope for this same forgiveness and healing. And yet, strangely, even when we do approach this Sacrament of forgiveness it can so easily just become part of our wider strategy to hide from the truth about ourselves. Our confession merely disguises our sins and deepens our alienation from God and from ourselves and from one another. Divine forgiveness is always a moment of truth about ourselves, a revelation that allows us at last to be at home in our adult world.

My child, your sins are forgiven. Jesus does not ask for the child's childish list and none is offered. For the man on the stretcher the time has come to be serious, the time at last for freedom from anxiety and self-concern and the paralysis to which they inevitably give rise, the time for commitment to life and to service of others.

What of the people who brought this man to Jesus, and the four neighbours who carried him on the stretcher? Theirs was a kind of desperate prayer that prepared the way for this astounding miracle in which the glory of God was revealed. It could be that our own prayers for those we know to be themselves beyond prayer are not sufficiently desperate to provoke such a miracle.

Isaiah 43:18-19. 21-22. 24-25 / Second Corinthians 1:18-22 / Mark 2:1-12

Tenth Sunday

Yes, the troubles which are soon over, though they weigh little, train us for the carrying of a weight of eternal glory which is out of all proportion to them.

Yes, brothers and sisters in Christ, if you could but see the weight of glory for which that person sitting beside you is in training it would distract you from my homily and indeed from any and all of your habitual distractions.

The big distraction in today's gospel, of course, is to explain who these people were who turned up claiming to be the brothers and sisters of Jesus. The real point is that his family, including his mother, were afraid he had gone over the top and wanted to take him home with them and look after him. They set out to take charge of him, convinced that he was out of his mind. But he insisted that he was already completely at home exactly where he was, with his disciples: Here are my mother and my brothers. Anyone who does the will of God, that person is my brother and sister and mother.

The first pages of the Bible give us a tantalizing glimpse of the family relationship that existed between God and humanity before the Fall. In the immediate aftermath of the Fall, in today's extract from Genesis, we find the first bewilderment of Adam and Eve at their self-inflicted exclusion from that easy familiarity with their Creator. God calls to them in the garden to know where they are and Adam has his first experience of shame and guilt. I heard the sound of you in the garden and I was afraid because I was naked, so I hid. And now the blame game takes off. It was the woman you put with me. She gave me the fruit and I ate it, he said and she said, The serpent tempted me and I ate.

But with the Lord there is mercy and fullness of redemption. God's plan to gather his human family together again is already fully formed in the divine mind. Yes, the troubles which are soon over, though they weigh little, will train his children for the carrying of a weight of eternal glory which is out of all proportion to them. The plan will cost, but the price will be paid. Jesus and his disciples, his brothers and sisters, will pay that price to the full but it will be worth it for they will know that when the tent they live in on earth is folded up, there is a house built by God for them, an everlasting family home, not made by human hands, in the heavens.

To claim to be a brother or sister of Jesus without doing the will of God is arguably the ultimate blasphemy against the Holy Spirit and it is hard to see how it might be forgiven.

Genesis 3:9-15 / Second Corinthians 4:31-5:1 / Mark 3:20-35

Eleventh Sunday

Jesus said: This is what the kingdom of God is like.

Behind the many tragedies of two thousand years of Christianity, brothers and sisters in Christ, we find again and again individuals or groups possessed by an absolute certainty about what the kingdom of God is like. It is surely a blessing if we ourselves are sometimes troubled by the suspicion that our own conviction about what the kingdom of God is like might not, after all, be the best way forward either for the Church in this time and place or even for ourselves and those whom life has entrusted to us. When the humble darkness of faith is displaced by blinding flashes of manic conviction disaster is not far behind.

This, said Jesus, is what the kingdom of God is like and he told his parables - parables that possess a peculiar authority for Jesus embodies their truth in his own person and the lifestyle that flows from it. When we listen to Jesus carefully, with our hearts rather than our heads, the light of that truth shines upon us and within us.

A man throws seed on the land and when the crop is ready, he loses no time: he starts to reap because the harvest has come. That is what the kingdom of God is like. There are certain steps we have to take to be part of it and we need to be ready to seize our moments of grace as they arise but for the rest we do well to be patient and learn to wait, and realise that what we are required to do is to do nothing at all. Night and day, while he sleeps, when he is awake, the seed is spouting and growing; how he does not know. Of its own accord the land produces first the shoot, then the ear, then the full grain in the ear.

The farmer is wise to do nothing. It is a way of doing by not doing, a profoundly respectful approach to life. It is a lesson of patience and humility that we do not easily learn. Our temptation is to dig up the seed every so often - just to be absolutely

sure that it is progressing satis-
factorily. Anxious concern is a
splendid recipe for failure. We learn
to care for ourselves and for others
by not caring too much. Interference,
impatience, trying too hard - these
are among the most subtle enemies
of the kingdom of God.

The kingdom comes in our lives
when three conditions are fulfilled:
firstly we are committed to seeking
God's will rather than our own,
secondly as a result of that
commitment we are ready to seize
our moments of grace as they occur
and thirdly we resolutely - and
patiently - leave the rest to God, we
resist every temptation to interfere,
we learn not to get in the way.

For the kingdom of God is like a
mustard seed which at the time of its
sowing in the soil is the smallest of
all the seeds on earth; yet once it is
sown it grows into the biggest shrub
of them all and puts out big branches
so that the birds of the air can shelter
in its shade.

We all have our little place in the great plan. We fail by trying too hard. We fail when we strive to be what we are not. God is patient with us and he invites us to be patient with ourselves and with one another. When a mustard seed has ambitions of its own it suffers pain and knows only frustration. There is a lack of shelter in the heat of the day - and the splendour of God's creation is diminished.

Ezekiel 17:22-24 / Second Corinthians 5:6-10 / Mark 4:26-34

Twelfth Sunday

Then it began to blow a gale and the waves were breaking into the boat so that it was almost swamped. But he was in the stern, his head on the cushion, asleep.

Serenity in the midst of a storm, brothers and sisters in Christ, is one of the more attractive qualities of the genuinely God-centred person. We have all perhaps experienced how easy it is to turn to God in moments of panic. What we want to know is the secret of Jesus that allows him to impose his inner calm upon every outward turmoil. Rather than turning to God in moments of panic, as even the pagans do, we sense how attractive it would be to imitate Jesus in his serenity.

After all, our moments of panic merely reveal the essential fear that is never far beneath the surface of our lives, the fact that however brave a face we might put on it we are not really at peace with ourselves. In the end it is not the drama of outward circumstances so much as the inner turmoil of our hearts and minds that brings shipwreck to our lives.

We sense the gap between the serenity of Jesus and the panic of his disciples. They woke him and said to him: Master, do you not care? We are going down. But he does care, and deeply, though about something else: Why are you so frightened? How is it that you have no faith?

The boat in the storm is a powerful image of our human lives pervaded by fear, for those whose lives are pervaded by fear are going down indeed. Why are you so frightened? How is it that you have no faith? These questions are addressed to us - and the tragedy of our lives is that we are so good at evading them. Fear is a kind of death. The more fear, the less life. As we struggle to survive against our fears we are not really alive. We are trapped in a kind of living death. Faith calms our fears and is the beginning of life.

Moments of panic may bring us to our knees but they do not bring us to

God. When panic passes and the seas of life recover their dull calmness we forget. We are not grateful to the God of panic. We tell ourselves it never really happened. We imagined it all.

Faith comes when at last we listen to a different God, the one who says to us: Be still and know that I am God. The disciples of Jesus did not then understand his stillness, his head on the cushion, asleep. But this is precisely the lesson that disciples learn. Their experience in the boat that day launched them in the right direction. They were filled with awe and said to one another: Who can this be? Even the wind and the sea obey him. To ponder that question, even in the midst of the storm, is to arrive at the stillness of faith and to know that God is God.

Job 3:1. 8-11 / Second Corinthians 5:14-17 / Mark 4:35-41

Thirteenth Sunday

Death was not God's doing, he takes no pleasure in the extinction of the living.

The thought of the unlived life, brothers and sisters in Christ, rightly fills us with horror. Some lives are cut short before they have half begun - like the daughter of Jairus in today's gospel, only twelve years old, desperately sick, her life in danger. Other lives are a sort of living death. That woman with the haemorrhage has lost twelve years of her life in a hopeless attempt to recover her health.

Yes, the thought of the unlived life rightly fills us with horror. And not least perhaps because the question arises for each one of us whether or not at this very moment our own life is being lived or left unlived.

While we are young and for as long as we flatter ourselves that we are still young we too easily put off beginning our lives until tomorrow.

As age creeps up on us so too perhaps does the suspicion that our death occurred some time ago. We see all around us the sadness of so many unlived lives, the young paralysed by fear of their future, the less young trapped by the mistakes of their past. Still, it need not be so. Life is meant to be lived. Such, at least, is the message of hope that is the Gospel of our Lord Jesus Christ.

Life can still be ours if we grasp hold of it today. We know well enough that this is not something we can achieve on our own. Jesus is the source of life. We can accept from him as a gift a fullness of life that we cannot even imagine much less achieve for ourselves. If we are paralysed by our fear of the future we can, like the daughter of Jairus, allow Jesus to take us by the hand and raise us up and send us on our way. If we are trapped by our past we can, like the woman with the haemorrhage, allow Jesus to heal us and give us back our lives. When at last life begins even the most horrendous past receives the gift of meaning, even the most daunting future can be faced with serenity.

Death was not God's doing, insists the Wisdom of the Old Testament, he takes no pleasure in the extinction of the living. The glory of God, says St Irenaeus in a memorable phrase, is a human being who is fully alive. Our living death is not God's will for us. Our failure to accept life is an affront to the God who offers us this wonderful gift. Jesus came to reveal the glory of the living God by being himself a man fully alive. He is the way, the truth and the life. He invites us to come to him in faith and accept the fullness of life. How perverse we are to waste our years in darkness when we are made in the image of God and called to be children of the light revealing his glory to the world as disciples of Jesus Christ, the Son of God, the first-born of many brothers and sisters.

Wisdom 1:13-15; 2:23-24 / Second Corinthians 8:7. 9. 13-15 / Mark 5:21-43

Fourteenth Sunday

A prophet is only despised in his own country, among his own relations and in his own house.

There are all kinds of reasons why people reject the message of Jesus, brothers and sisters in Christ, but surely there is none more unexpected and indeed astounding than the reason why the people of Nazareth refuse to accept him: they know who he is. He might have looked forward to a special welcome in his native place. We might have thought that Nazareth would be the privileged scene of his most spectacular conversions. They are impressed by his wisdom and his miracles but their reaction is negative and mean-spirited: Where did the man get all this? What is this wisdom that has been granted to him, and these miracles that are worked thorough him?

What have they against him, we might wonder. They have nothing against his words and his deeds as such: they are the words and deeds of a man of God. They have nothing against him personally, the man they have known for thirty years as one of themselves, the carpenter, the son of Mary. What they cannot take is the fact that this man of God with his gift of preaching and his power to heal should be one and the same with the carpenter, the son of Mary whom they thought they knew all about. It is not acceptable, indeed it is scandalous, that one of themselves should stand up and stand out as something more than what they had always taken him to be. They cannot and will not understand that one of themselves has been called to stand up and stand out as the messenger of God. They are waiting for a Messiah and they are very sure that Jesus of Nazareth is not and cannot be that Messiah because, quite simply, they know all about him. Jesus himself is amazed at their lack of faith and he can work no miracle among them.

What we could learn from this for ourselves is that this same tragic thing happens with us all the time. We have long ago made up our

minds about the people around us -
the members of our family, our
friends, our neighbours, the people
we work with. We know them inside
out. We know what to expect from
them and too often we don't expect
very much. In the same way very
probably we have made up our
minds about what we can expect of
ourselves and what we can expect of
God. And all that too probably
doesn't add up to very much.

Today's gospel shows us Jesus
coming to his home town. Because
they are so sure that they know who
he is, he himself is unable to convey
to them who he really is. It is the
tragic story of day God came to
Nazareth and passed on unnoticed.
They were not ready to find the truly
extraordinary in the totally ordinary -
and sadly neither are we.

The total ordinariness of Jesus
invites us and challenges us to find
the extraordinary things of God in
the ordinary things of our own everyday lives. Jesus invites us and
challenges us to be free of this
prejudice that we have, once and for

all, taken the measure of one another, of our own lives and of God. We are free to give one another another chance. We are free to give ourselves another chance. We are free to give God another chance.

At Nazareth that day there was one small, almost insignificant group who did give Jesus his chance and it was not in vain. As Mark tells us, he could work no miracle there, though he cured a few sick people by laying his hands on them. As Paul says, it is when I am weak that I am strong. When we are too sure that we know it all God passes us by a thousand times every day.

Ezekiel 2:2-5 / Second Corinthians 12:7-10 /Mark 6:1-6

Fifteenth Sunday

And he instructed them to take nothing for the journey.

Today's gospel, brothers and sisters in Christ, has a strangeness about it that unsettles us. Somehow we feel that what is strange here should in fact be familiar. Certainly it is all very strange. It is so unlike anything that is immediately familiar to us. We are tempted to dismiss it as a bizarre exercise that Jesus set for his first disciples but if we dare to ask what it might have to say to us today we might be surprised. What if this exercise were not an end in itself but the beginning of something really great that has gone on uninterrupted ever since? Jesus summoned the Twelve, Mark tells us, and began to send them out in pairs giving them authority over the unclean spirits. He gives them certain instructions for the journey and they set off to preach repentance. They cast out many devils and heal many sick people.

Unclean spirits, devils to be cast out - all this is indeed strange to us, or is it? Are we not all too familiar with the fears and anxieties, the complexes and the neuroses that take possession of people as much today as ever before causing so much mental and physical anguish? If we have the courage to look into our own hearts we might find how little authority we have over our own unclean spirits. Are we as self-possessed as we would like to think, or are we possessed by something else over which we have little or no control?

For two thousand years now the messengers of Jesus have been travelling the highways and byways of the world with his authority over unclean spirits and preaching his message of repentance. Some will say that it has not been very effective. Surely the thing could have been done more thoroughly. The business could have been much better organised. A more energetic approach might have been employed.

Looking back to today's gospel however we have to recognize that the instructions of Jesus are quite explicit. The disciples are to take nothing for the journey and they are not to pay any heed to how they are received. Who is to say that they have not been successful in their mission? Have not all other strategies and techniques proved self-defeating?

The messengers of Jesus are to take nothing for the journey: that is to say if they impress those they meet along the way it will not be because of what they have but because of what they are. They will not trick others into conversion by appearing to be something that they are not. They will touch them by the simplicity of what they genuinely are. In the eyes of the world they will not be spectacularly successful in their mission. They will take people as they are. They will share themselves with those who welcome them. They will not force themselves on those who do not. Nor will they waste their time with them. They simply pass on. They know that God is not in a hurry. He does not need to use force. It is counterproductive for his messengers in the world to be in a hurry to succeed, to be discouraged by apparent failure, to be tempted to use force on God's behalf.

There are too many people in today's world who do not believe in Jesus because of the violent and authoritarian way the Christian message has so often been presented. No one can be forced to believe, no one can be tricked into belief. If we really want to share our Christian faith with others we must first have a most holy respect for them and go out to meet them in a simple, genuine, gentle and patient way. When we dare to do that we will find ourselves set free from our own unclean spirits.

Amos 7:12-15 / Ephesians 1:3-14 / Mark 6:7-13

Sixteenth Sunday

The Lord is my shepherd.

This most beloved of Psalms, brothers and sisters in Christ, is the prayer of a pilgrim allowing the Lord to guide him along the right path. Jesus took pity on the crowd because they were like sheep without a shepherd. It was nothing new. Already Jeremiah and Ezekiel had conveyed God's criticism of the shepherds of Israel. Doom for the shepherds who allow the flock of my pasture to be destroyed and scattered. You have allowed my flock to be scattered and go wandering and have not taken care of them.

The Lord is my shepherd: Near restful waters he leads me to revive my drooping spirit. Until we turn to the Lord to look for shepherding the chances are that we have been fol-lowing all kinds of other shepherds. We have carelessly chosen our own false shepherds who have led us astray. The mark of the false shepherd is that he exploits the crowd for his own advantage. The false shepherds of today are trained in manipulation and exploitation - with our complicity. They are at work at every level of public and private life - with our complicity. It is comfortable in the crowd. There are so many ways in which we prefer to lose ourselves rather than enter upon or continue the spiritual journey to the truth of who we are. For that takes courage and confidence in God: If I should walk in the valley of darkness no evil would I fear. You are there with your crook and your staff, with these you give me comfort.

The Lord is my shepherd. There is nothing I shall want. This is a prayer guaranteed to put the false shepherds to flight for it is the mark of the false shepherd that he bent on selling us something. It is a prayer that says: No thank you, false shepherd. The Lord is my shepherd. There is nothing I shall want.

A large crowd pursues Jesus and his disciples in today's gospel. People saw them going and many could guess where and from every town they all hurried to the place on foot and reached it before them. That crowd was fortunate that it happened to be Jesus they were pursuing. He took pity on them because they were like sheep without a shepherd and he set himself to teach them at some length. Often we are less fortunate in the crowds we choose to get lost in. False shepherds encourage us to merge with the crowd, their crowd, and disappear. They may use many words and employ every technique of rhetoric and sophistry but they have nothing life-giving to teach us. The good shepherd, in contrast, invites us to emerge from the crowd, to honour our own uniqueness, to find ourselves, to become who we are called to be.

You must come away to some lonely place all by yourselves, he tells us, and rest for a while. Fresh and green are the pastures where he gives me repose. The good shepherd seeks the one who is lost. Each one of us lost in the crowd he cares for and he calls us, each one of us, by our own name until we come to him - so that his crowd is no longer a crowd, no longer sheep without a shepherd, but a community, a community of shepherds caring for one another.

Yes, in Jesus the good shepherd we become shepherds to one another. It is the fulfilment in the Christian community of God's ancient promise: the remnant of my flock I myself will gather from all the countries where I have dispersed them, and will bring them back to their pastures: they shall be fruitful and increase in numbers. I will raise up shepherds to look after them and pasture them; no fear, no terror for them any more; not one shall be lost - it is the Lord who speaks.

The Lord is my shepherd. There is nothing I shall want. Surely goodness and kindness shall follow me all the days of my life. In the Lord's own house shall I dwell for ever and ever. Amen.

Jeremiah 23:1-6 / Ephesians 2:13-18 / Mark 6:30-34

Seventeenth Sunday

This really is the prophet who is to come into the world.

Nowadays, brothers and sisters in Christ, we understand better than earlier generations the veil of projection that separates us from the truth. We know that we see everything through the distortions of our own previous experiences and the prejudices of the communities to which we belong. We are not, then, surprised that the people who saw the sign of the loaves and fish at the Sea of Galilee that day could rightly identify Jesus as the prophet who was to come into the world and yet at the same time so grossly misconceive his purpose that he had to flee from them. He could see that they were about to come and take him by force and make him king, the gospel tells us, and so he escaped back to the hills by himself. We are therefore alert to the real possibility that however genuine our own faith we are in danger of so misunderstanding Jesus that as often as we try

48

to lay hold of him it is all he can do to run away from us.

Jesus took the loaves, gave thanks, and gave them out to all who were sitting ready; he then did the same with the fish, giving out as much as was wanted. It is an unmistakeably Eucharistic sign for at the Last Supper too Jesus took and, thanking God, gave to the disciples sitting with him the bread and wine become his body and blood for the salvation of the world. And as we do that today as he commanded us in memory of him, proclaiming the mystery of our faith in him and saying Amen to him in Holy Communion, the tragedy of the people in this Gospel text alerts us to the danger we ourselves run of missing the point of the Eucharist - regardless of the precision of our belief and the sincerity of our commitment.

The letter to the Ephesians reminds us that belief and commitment are measured by their fruit. The author implores us across the centuries to lead a life worthy of our calling. And he does not hesitate to spell it out for us. Those who believe in Jesus and are committed to a Eucharistic lifestyle bear with one another charitably, in complete selflessness, gentleness and patience doing all they can to preserve the unity of the Spirit by the peace that binds them together.

We can be sure that we have missed the point of the Eucharist if we find ourselves explaining away our deviations from the Eucharistic lifestyle, our lack of tolerance, our failure to forgive, our obsession with ourselves, our aggression, our impatience. For Jesus came to set us free from all such compromises by involving us in the mystery of his death and resurrection. When we confess our sins we admit that we have not yet made that freedom fully own but that we still intend to do so. In the Mass we express our faith and renew our commitment.

Jesus nourishes, strengthens and encourages us as we persevere in our journey towards the fullness of truth and freedom.

Sundays in Ordinary Time – Year B

Second Kings 4:42-44 / Ephesians 4:1-6 / John 6:1-15

Eighteenth Sunday

Your mind must be renewed by a spiritual revolution so that you can put on the new self that has been created in God's way, in the goodness and holiness of the truth.

Revolution, brothers and sisters in Christ, is never an attractive option for people who are comfortable. The hidden hope in the aimless kind of life that pagans live is that it can end up being very boring or at least sufficiently uncomfortable to inspire in us a vague desire for something more. There must be something more, we sometimes find ourselves saying - and that heartfelt suspicion is the seed of a spiritual revolution that can launch us on a journey out of darkness into light. We begin to dismantle our old self and await the gift of the new self, created in God's way, in the goodness and holiness of the truth.

We would all agree, I imagine, that Jesus preaches and embodies a way of life that we find attractive. We might sometimes wonder why it is that we never quite get round to making it our own. It does not easily occur to us to attribute our failure to our attachment to our old self which, as Ephesians reminds us, gets corrupted by following illusory desires. You must give up your old way of life: it is hard for us to think of this imperative as addressed directly to us. We think more readily of others who in our view could well do with giving up their old way of life. Perhaps we cannot really feel that there is much wrong with the aimless kind of life that pagans live. Or perhaps we cover our own aimlessness in a cloak of religious respectability that fools only our-selves. Or perhaps indeed we have given up our old way of life and been so pleased about it that we have forgotten that it is a challenge to be faced again and again until the day we die.

Until we are ready for the spiritual revolution that Christian discipleship involves we remain the victims of our illusory desires. Unconscious victims, unaware of our captivity, comfortable in our illusions. Perhaps the words that Jesus addresses to the crowd that pursued him after the miracle of the loaves and fish today intrude upon our dreams and unsettle us in a healthy sort of way: I tell you most solemnly, you are not looking for me because you have seen the signs but because you had all the bread you wanted to eat. Do not work for food that cannot last, but for food that endures to eternal life, the kind of food the Son of Man is offering you, for on him the Father, God himself, has set his seal.

Do not work for food that cannot last. Give up your old way of life. Put aside your old self, which gets corrupted by following illusory desires. Work instead for food that endures to eternal life. We can of course go on living the aimless kind of life that pagans live. But we risk missing the point of life itself. Perhaps we have failed to hear Jesus properly in the past. Today he invites us once again to address the challenge of our own personal spiritual revolution. I am the bread of life, he assures us. He who comes to

me will never be hungry. He who
believes in me will never thirst.

Exodus 16:2-4. 12-15 / Ephesians 4:17. 20-24 / John 6:24-35

Nineteenth Sunday

Elijah went into the wilderness, a day's journey, and sitting under a furze bush he wished he were dead.

Depression, brothers and sisters in Christ, is a common and very human experience that has the profoundest religious significance.

Elijah expresses the core of that experience in all its personal drama. Lord, he said, I have had enough. Take my life. I am no better than my ancestors. Elijah's experience of depression is typical. He can make no sense of himself. He sees no meaning in his continued existence. He is no use to others. He is a burden to himself. It would be better all round if he were dead.

Those who suffer from depression are privileged in a religious sense for their keen realisation of the triviality of so much that passes for important in life awakens them to their need for God. Their misfortune is that overwhelmed by their failure to prove their love for God they lose sight of God's unconditional love for them. Their own attempts at love are so desperate that they never realise just how much they themselves are loved. They can never do enough for others. Indeed they find it almost impossible to say no to the often thoughtless demands that are made on them. Spiritual healing can only begin when they come to see that their real sin is not their failure to be helpful and useful to all and sundry but rather the simple fact that they try much too hard. After all a little real generosity has more practical effect in the real world than a vain fantasy of permanent readiness for total sacrifice.

Elijah tried too hard. Elijah failed. Elijah fell into depression. He had had enough. He sat down under a furze bush and wished he were dead. In his desperate attempt to prove his love for God he had forgotten how much God loved him. He needed a gentle reminder of that love. Without that gentle reminder he would indeed have slept the sleep of death, dehydrated by the desert sun, the prey of passing vultures. For that is so often the fate of the depressed – wearied and parched, exploited and victimised, they wither and die.

Elijah lay down and went to sleep - but an angel touched him and said: Get up and eat. A scone baked on hot stones and a jar of water. It was not much and Elijah did not see the point of it. He ate and drank and then lay down again. The fog of depression is like that. It is its own bulwark against every kindness. But the angel of the Lord came back a second time and touched him and said: Get up and eat, or the journey will be too long for you. What journey? Elijah was persuaded that there was no-where for him to go, that his life was over, that he had no further meaning or purpose to live for. But touched again by the gentle kindness of God he got up and ate and drank, and strengthened by that food he walked for forty days and forty nights until he reached Horeb, the mountain of God.

The journey to the mountain of God is a long journey and often a lonely journey but not to face it is to die in the wilderness, of no use to others and a burden to ourselves. Today we come once again to the Eucharist to seek sustenance for our journey. Today we come once again to Jesus, the bread of life.

Let us not grieve the Holy Spirit of God who has marked us with his seal for us to be set free when the day comes.

First Kings 19:4-8 / Ephesians 4:30 – 5:2 / John 6:41-51

Twentieth Sunday

Be very careful about the sort of lives you lead, like intelligent and not like senseless people. This may be a wicked age, but your lives should redeem it.

Wisdom, brothers and sisters in Christ, is a word one rarely hears nowadays. In the ancient world in which the Bible texts were born wisdom was highly prized as a divine gift. To be wise was to have gathered something about the meaning of life from one's experiences. The wise man or woman was the one who knew what was important, the person who knew how to rise above the changing circumstances of their life and be happy. Wisdom was a divine gift, a sign of divine favour, the ultimate purpose and goal of true religion.

The wise emerge from the foolish crowd. There have always been fools, of course, senseless people who waste their time and energy, and squander their resources. Those who drug themselves in one way or another against the pain of life's challenges and run after the false wisdom of whatever false prophets happen to be the heroes of the moment. It is the question about happiness. The wise person quite simply knows how to be happy, here and now, regardless of their personal circumstances. The fool looks forward to being happy, or clings to some distorted memory of past happiness.

We can often recognize the gift of wisdom in those who have been graced by it. To know such people is to be oneself a little wiser. We have no difficulty in identifying fools and we can surely learn from their foolishness. But when we look into our own heart it is not quite so easy for us to say whether we are wise or foolish for it is in our heart that the eternal battle between wisdom and folly is fought out.

And while we live in this world the temptation of folly, the fascination of foolishness is never fully vanquished. Perhaps indeed the ultimate foolishness is that of the self-righteous, the Pharisee in all of us, our facility for believing with such charming naivety and sincerity that we are right and good and that everyone else is more or less wayward and wrong. To be gifted with wisdom is to know that today we will learn something new about ourselves, about our fellow human beings and about God himself. Fools, characteristically, know it all already. They have nothing to learn. But just as the wise embody a fragile gift so too the situation of the foolish is not without hope.

To the fool wisdom says: Come and eat my bread, drink the wine I have prepared! Leave your folly and you will live, walk in the ways of perception. Jesus said to the crowd: I am the living bread which has come down from heaven. Anyone who eats this bread will live for ever. And the bread that I shall give is my flesh for the life of the world.

It is foolish to receive the bread of life without knowing what it is for. The redemption of the age we live in advances a little further with every human heart that is touched by wisdom.

Proverbs 9:1-6 / Ephesians 5:15-20 / John 6:51-58

Twenty-First Sunday

We too will serve the Lord, for he is our God.

Commitment, brothers and sisters in Christ, is an increasingly difficult concept. There must be a deal of ambiguity in any commitment that hardens into stubbornness. An overly stubborn commitment is the enemy of good religion and there are enough examples of it. There is too a certain contemporary mentality that questions the very possibility of an open-ended commitment of any kind and gives rise, at best, to a kind of religious tourism.

Commitment to religious practices that are genuinely spiritual cannot but lead the believer in the direction of God. The Catholic forms of Christian commitment are tried and tested. The commitment to daily prayer. The commitment to the Sunday Eucharist and to the right observance of Sunday. The commitment to Friday penance. The commitment to honesty and generosity in everyday life. The commitment to making a full confession of our sins at least once a year. It is by our fidelity to these commitments that we grow in spiritual freedom.

Christian marriage is one form of this freedom that is particularly threatened by the general collapse of commitment in the pagan society around us. The secret of Christian marriage was always that when the infatuation of romantic attraction evaporated, as it inevitably must, the commitment to that one other person for better or for worse, for richer or for poorer, in sickness and in health remained as the solid basis for a personal freedom where love took on an entirely new meaning. In an ambient culture that trivialises human sexuality this Christian commitment to marriage is a beacon of hope, a beacon fuelled not only by the Christian fidelity of husbands and wives but also by the Christian chastity of the rest of us. A beacon of hope indeed in a sad world that has lost the script for human happiness.

We cannot camouflage the presence of the cross at the heart of our commitments in the Christian way of life. Jesus spoke the language of the cross and to many who heard him it was intolerable language. They walked with him no more, like a certain rich young man who went away sad. The rich, the famous and the beautiful continue to walk away in droves, most indeed without much perceptible trace of immediate sadness. But Jesus does not modify his tone. He simply repeats, as gently as he can: It is the spirit that gives life, the flesh has nothing to offer. The words I have spoken to you are spirit and they are life.

When we stumble over the cross at the heart of our own commitments we too are tempted to walk away. But Simon Peter, as always, speaks for our truest selves: Lord, to whom shall we go? You have the message of eternal life. And we believe: we know that you are the Holy One of God.

Joshua 24:1-2. 15-18 / Ephesians 5:21-32 / John 6:60-69

Twenty-Second Sunday

But you must do what the word tells you, and not just listen to it and deceive yourselves.

Hypocrisy, brothers and sisters in Christ, is not an entirely deliberate vice. It is a largely unconscious exercise in self-deception. It starts off from the conviction that what other people think of us is ultimately more important than the truth about ourselves. And we end by ourselves believing the lie behind which we have camouflaged our truth.

Jesus came to set us free from our lies about ourselves and help us face our truth. He is not concerned with our table manners or our respect for social conventions. Or rather he is concerned that we might think those things important. He fears for us that we might think we are worshipping God when we are merely entangled in lip-service unaware of the gulf that separates us from the true God and our true selves. He fears for us that we might have had our reward already. For hypocrisy does indeed have its own rewards and they are tangible enough. It is a way of getting on in the world, at a price we think we can afford because, of course, it does not have to be paid - just yet.

Pure, unspoilt religion, in the eyes of God our Father, is something else altogether. It is about coming to the help of those in need and keeping ourselves uncontaminated by the world. Naturally there is a certain prudence to be exercised in how we use our resources in helping those in need and there is a right way as well as a wrong way of relating to the world. But it is always an illusion to suppose that we have achieved these insights once and for all. There is a sad and inconsequential way of listening to wisdom that does not involve us in doing anything - except deceiving ourselves. Real listening bears fruit. It stirs us into action and leads to radical change.

Hypocrisy is essentially concern about how we look from the outside. Once we know how we should look our temptation is to cultivate the right image, in a grotesque display of charity and devotion. There are rewards for appearing to be religious. Generosity and detachment can be faked. The message of religion is that how we look from outside does not matter at all.

What matters is the heart. Often when we say about someone that their heart is in the right place it is merely a patronizing way of excusing their ineffectiveness or their silliness. But when someone's heart is really in the right place there is nothing ineffective or silly about them, but instead real wisdom to be admired. It is how we look from the inside that counts. And for those who have wasted their lives worrying about how they look from the outside it requires the most extraordinary courage to look inward and face the truth and begin to empty their heart of the clutter of a lifetime.

Jesus offers us the courage that we need and guarantees the freedom that will be our reward. Every time we come to Mass Jesus renews the invitation of our Baptism to enter fully into the mystery of his cross and resurrection - by purifying our hearts before God rather than worrying about how we look to others.

Is it really such a difficult choice this, between the reward that satisfies our vanity and the reward that rescues our souls from death?

Deuteronomy 4:1-2. 6-8 / James 1:17-18. 21-22. 27 / Mark 7:1-8. 14-15. 21-23

Twenty-Third Sunday

And they brought him a deaf man who had an impediment in his speech.

Today's gospel, brothers and sisters in Christ, is about a man not gifted in speech and shut off from the voices around him. In our own way we too can be a little hard of hearing at times and we do not always make the best use of our tongues. Indeed when it comes to what really matters we are, all of us, strangely deaf and tongue-tied.

We too need to be taken away from the crowd for our healing. For we are more deaf than ever in a crowd where everyone is shouting. We find no words of our own in a crowd where nobody is listening. We get comfortable with our life in the crowd, though it leaves us deaf and speechless. It is the way we have grown over the years, what we have learnt about how to survive.

And as often as we in our turn have made a child to be silent because it did not suit us to listen we have added to the loveless indifference of the crowd and left it harder for an adult years later to tell their truth. For it is only by being listened to that we learn to speak. It is only in trying to speak our own truth that we learn to listen to others and support them in speaking theirs.

Jesus took the man aside, in private, away from the crowd. He touched him and prayed and said to him: Ephphata, be opened. And his ears were opened and he spoke clearly - for the first time, his nightmare ended. Ephphata. Be opened. Courageous words that we too are called to speak to one another. But we do not dare to utter such words. Anything might happen, and deep down we are afraid of miracles.

Jesus has shown us how to treat one another with respect and love. He has shown us a way of being with people in pain, a way of listening and sharing and touching that heals. We recognize in Jesus the fullness of our own humanity and when we imitate him our world becomes a more gracious and a more compassionate place, a place of welcome where we can all be at home with one another and speak our truth in love.

But we remain strangely deaf and tongue-tied. We have no ears for the whispers of love around us. We have no voice to speak our better feelings. We wait for Jesus to touch us with his healing, Jesus who makes the deaf hear and the dumb speak - for the glory of God and the salvation of the world.

Isaiah 35:4-7 / James 2:1-5 / Mark 7:31-37

Twenty-Fourth Sunday

But you, he said, who do you say I am?

The question of who Jesus is, brothers and sisters in Christ, is not a question that can be answered once and for all. It is, rather, a question that accompanies us on our journey through life. We catch glimpses. We garner fragments. But we never have the full picture. The words of Jesus reach out to us from today's gospel and challenge us directly and personally: You, he says, who do you say I am?

It is somehow an awkward question. But then do we ever really know another person? Do we ever really know ourselves? Who are you? Who am I? - these are the basic questions that reveal the meaning of our lives. From the moment we are born to the moment we die we are constantly being told who we are. We all have to face it: chatter, gossip, prejudice, and stereotyping, conditioning and tradition - there is no escape for any of us. Peter does to Jesus exactly what we so often do to one another. He does not like the sound of what Jesus is saying. He interrupts with remonstration.

And in this he finds a following down through the centuries in the sentimentality and comforting clap-trap of those who revolt at the hard word of the cross. Their way of thinking is not God's way but man's. And we must be resolute in evading them. For everything is at stake. Get behind me, Satan! You are an obstacle in my path.

Peter, with all his fair words and fine feelings, is more ready to say who he would like Jesus to be than to accept the truth of who Jesus actually is, what it really means for him to be the Christ. The cobwebs of Peter's human thought-patterns have not yet been blown away by the mystery of the cross. His heart is still set on some kind of worldly success rather than the fulfilment of the mysterious purposes of God.

There is something of this in all of us. We are always caught somewhere between God's way and our own. But as we identify our cross and begin to shoulder it, we sense that there are no short cuts, no easy exits. If anyone wants to be a follower of mine, says Jesus, let them renounce themself and take up their cross and follow me. He says it to each one of us, yes, at the most crucial moments of our lives. And this law of the cross is the law of life itself.

A truly fulfilled life eludes the grasp of those who purposefully seek self-fulfilment. Only those who cease to grasp at life, only those who abandon their own petty projects for a customized, made-to-measure passage through this world, only those who surrender themselves to God in imitation of Jesus, only they will enter into the fullness of life, only they will discover who Jesus really is, only they will ever know who they really are themselves.

The alternative is just too terrible to contemplate.

Sundays in Ordinary Time – Year B

Isaiah 50:5-9 / James 2:14-18 / Mark 8:27-35

Twenty-Fifth Sunday

Why you don't have what you want is because you don't pray for it. When you do pray and don't get it, it is because you have not prayed properly. You have prayed for something to indulge your own desires.

True prayer, brothers and sisters in Christ, brings us into the presence of God and transforms our lives. Of course we pray in moments of crisis when we have really nowhere else to turn. That can be a useful introduction to prayer. But it is not yet true prayer. True prayer is a long term project that leads us from false notions about ourselves and the world along an often painful path of detachment and purification until we reach a certain peace in the presence of God.

Today's gospel shows us how difficult the disciple's journey can be. The time has come for Jesus to prepare his disciples for what is soon to happen to him, his suffering, death and resurrection. They don't understand and are afraid to ask. They have preoccupations of their own: which of them is the greatest? It is an exceptionally embarrassing moment. Jesus preaches a greatness-in-service which is unpalatable to the world but nevertheless the price of discipleship. If anyone wants to be first he must make himself last of all and the servant of all. To welcome a child in his name is to welcome Jesus and the one who sent him. All too often the welcoming of children and the other little ones of our society is sacrificed in the pursuit of some personal greatness as the world understands it.

The reversal of personal priorities that Jesus preaches has prompted much compassion and goodness in the world. We all admire it when we see it. Do we admire it enough to want to be part of it? And when we have reached that point is there anything else worth praying for? We have all come here today with our own preoccupations. Perhaps a moment's reflection is enough to show us how unworthy those preoccupations are. Or perhaps our absorption in ourselves is so great that we are not really here at all. Nothing could be more ordinary than that, this failure to be present to ourselves in the here and now. It is the very thing Jesus came to save us from. In the Mass he tries once again and with infinite patience to draw us into the mystery of his suffering, death and resurrection, to lead us a little further into discipleship so that we die a little more to our own silliness and embody a little more that compassion and goodness that we admire so much when we see them in others.

Our prayer is the instrument of this ongoing, long-term transformation. Learning to pray properly involves painful disappointments at every stage. At first we feel that our prayers are not answered. But prayer always is answered and for the beginner in prayer the most common answer is the one suggested to us today by the letter of James: You have not prayed properly. You have prayed for something to indulge your own desires. Of course we are deaf to this answer. If we could even hear ourselves we would quickly realise how foolish our prayers sometimes are. We know better than God. Always. The whole thrust of our prayer is to persuade God to change his mind. But God does not change his mind: You have not prayed properly. You have prayed for something to indulge your own desires.

True prayer does not change God. It changes us. Slowly and painfully. Thy Kingdom come. Thy will be done. Deliver us from evil. True prayer leads us at last to true peace, a peace that allows us to welcome Jesus in all God's children and to welcome God himself in all the circumstances of our lives.

Wisdom 2:12. 17-20 / James 3:16 – 4:3 / Mark 9:30-37

Twenty-Sixth Sunday

It was a burning fire that you stored up as your treasure for the last days.

The Bible, brothers and sisters in Christ, has had a notable influence on the way we express ourselves. It has given us words for all kinds of everyday situations and circumstances. We often forget where such sayings and phrases come from. Today's gospel reminds us of a particularly nasty little expression it might be as well to forget, if only we could live without it. Yes, there it is in today's gospel, and twice. We saw a man who is 'not one of us' ... and because he was 'not one of us' we tried to stop him. Yes, 'not one of us'..., can we even begin to explain who's who among us without using this sectarian euphemism that comes to us directly from the pages of the Bible.

Goodness and kindness and decency are the work of the Holy Spirit of God - wherever they are found. The disciples of Jesus have no monopoly on grace and any Christian group that imagines it can claim such a monopoly does no service to the Gospel. We are to recognize the work of grace wherever we come across it and give thanks to God for it - unreservedly and with all our hearts. Anyone who is not against us is for us, says Jesus. It is the wisdom of common sense. And Jesus has harsh words for those who are off-message on this one. They are an obstacle to faith and they would be better thrown into the sea with a great millstone around their neck. For there can be no greater sin than to block another person's path to God.

And we can do no greater damage to ourselves than to block our own path to God. For when we block our own path to God we create our own personal hell. We become our own worst enemies. We close our hearts to grace. We refuse the risk of faith. We grasp hold of our little world with our own two hands. We stand firm on our own two feet. We stare out at the world through our own two eyes. And what have we got?

Until we risk everything in the simplicity of faith we will never know what it is to receive all we need from the hands of a loving Father. We will never know what it is to be supported and carried by the Holy Spirit of that love. We will never know what it is to see all things with those eyes of love that alone can conquer our blind indifference.

For as long as we continue to use our hands only to grasp at what we want, for as long as we continue to use our feet only to dig our heels in, for as long as we continue to use our eyes only to confirm our limited view of the world, for that long, and it can be an eternity, we will continue scornfully to dismiss as 'not one of us', anyone who has let go and allowed themselves to be carried into the light, surrendering that wilful independence of hand and foot and eye that is such an obstacle to faith.

The real sadness is that we are 'not one of them' - for in their freedom they have become the hands and feet of Jesus in this world, his eyes and

ears and voice, the instruments of his
love and joy and peace.

*Numbers 11:25-29 / James 5:1-6 / Mark
9:38-43. 45. 47-48*

Twenty-Seventh Sunday

This is why a man leaves his father and mother and joins himself to his wife, and they become one body.

The mystery of human sexuality, brothers and sisters in Christ, is celebrated in both the Jewish and the Christian tradition with a particular joy and lightness of heart. The creation story in the opening pages of the Bible enshrines a powerful love-song from three thousand years ago that rivals many more recent lyrics: This at last is bone from my bones, and flesh from my flesh. The author of Genesis recognizes that it is not good for a man or woman to be alone. We are incomplete without the companionship that marriage offers. And although Jesus will say that a great many of his followers are called to accept and live this incompleteness for the sake of the kingdom, marriage remains for most people a large part of the normal path to holiness.

This is why a man leaves his father and mother and joins himself to his wife, and they become one body. This ancient biblical statement that Jesus repeats in his rejection of divorce reveals a great deal about the true nature of marriage. Marriage is certainly not for children. It is not for the faint-hearted. It is, rather, for adults who have taken a genuine step in the direction of maturity by leaving childhood behind, by leaving father and mother - not just by moving house, so to speak, but in the sense of a growing beyond the emotional ties of childhood.

Marriages often fail where a man or woman is still looking really for the comfort of a mother's or a father's love, rather than the challenge of a mature adult relationship in which husband and wife become one with each other for life. Marriages are often undermined by a childish emotional dependency that has never developed into mature commitment to this one other person, for better, for worse, for richer, for poorer, in sickness and in health, as long as they both shall live.

To speak of failure in marriage is, of course, to raise the question about divorce. Jesus is not saying, and the Church after him does not say, that marriages can be made to work by forcing people to stay together. Where marriages last it is because love is mature. This maturity develops over time. It never comes to those who give up too quickly. The Church has always encouraged married couples in difficulty to try again, while at the same time bowing to the reality of marital breakdown.

Looking at the broader picture we sometimes wonder what it means for us to be faithful to this teaching of Jesus in a world that proposes so many alternative solutions to the human need not to be alone. How are we to live ourselves? And how are we to relate to those whose options, however socially acceptable in the pagan world around us, are at variance with the demands of Christian chastity and Christian witness?

We have a responsibility to seek answers that do justice to our own discipleship. Smugness, harshness and indifference are common but inappropriate reactions, not least, in regard to members of our own families. We are called to compassion and concern. And, above all, we are called to witness: the witness of a genuine chastity in our own particular life situation that fully respects the mystery of human sexuality in ourselves and others, the witness of a genuine chastity that fully respects the promises that we and others have made in the very presence of God himself.

Genesis 2:18-24 / Hebrews 2:9-11 / Mark 10:2-16

Twenty-Eight Sunday

But his face fell at these words and he went away sad, for he was a man of great wealth.

We do not know what became of him afterwards, brothers and sisters in Christ, but certainly this was not his moment of grace. His story unsettles us. We see ourselves in his position. We too would like to know from Jesus what we must do to inherit eternal life. We too keep most of the commandments most of the time and we were thinking perhaps that we were doing well enough. It unsettles us, this suggestion that something more might be required of us.

And then there is this question about our money. We don't like questions about money. It is an embarrassing subject. We would prefer not to think of money as a religious issue at all. Give the money to the poor, he said, and you will have treasure in heaven. Not a very sensible idea, not very practical. We share the astonishment of those first disciples. But Jesus is adamant: It is easier for a camel to pass through the eye of a needle than for a rich man to enter the kingdom of God.

Good master, what must I do to inherit eternal life? We sense the enthusiasm and urgency behind the question and we identify with it. It is already a great deal to want an answer to this question. We spend long periods of our lives indifferent to such questions and many never get round to asking them at all. What must I do to inherit eternal life? You know the commandments, Jesus replies. Yes, that too is a great deal, to be concerned with how we relate to other people so as to do them no wrong. But is it really enough?

There is one thing you lack, Jesus tells him. Yes, from us too something more is required: a certain detachment from everything that comes between us and discipleship. It is not always easy to identify exactly what it is that keeps us from following Jesus in perfect freedom and even when we have got as far as recognizing what it is in our own case we baulk at the final step. Our face falls and we go away sad for it is all just too much for us.

Why do we go away sad? It is essentially because in the end we are more concerned with what we have than with who we are. We cling to our great wealth, whatever form it takes, because it masks our radical poverty and defencelessness. For many it is in fact a straight-forward question of money and property. But the case of those who seek their security elsewhere is not very different. We become the slaves of whatever we put our trust in. The freedom of the disciple is to know that in the end there is no security in human life.

When we acknowledge our own absolute poverty before God we free our hearts and our resources however limited for the service of those less fortunate than ourselves. Wealth of whatever kind can be put to good use in a world of human suffering. It will not buy us a place in heaven but the fact that we are able to part with it is a sign of our freedom. It is no secret that wealth that is hoarded isolates and imprisons its victims.

Those who do give up everything to follow Jesus are freed from that burden and admitted to a fellowship that is a foretaste of eternal life.

Wisdom 7:7-11 / Hebrews 4:12-13 / Mark 10:17-30

Twenty-Ninth Sunday
Mission Sunday

We must never let go of the faith that we have professed.

On Mission Sunday, brothers and sisters in Christ, the Church focuses our attention on all those whose vocation it is to bring the message of the Gospel to the furthest ends of the earth. We are reminded to pray for them, to support them financially and to encourage them. Many of us know such missionaries personally and it is no small thing that we keep in touch with them and take an interest in what they are doing. The Irish contribution to the foreign missions - as they used to be called - was for the best part of a century nothing short of spectacular though these last decades have been a time of transition and withdrawal.

But mission begins at home. In the Ireland of today religion has become a matter of indifference to a great many people. We are constantly being told that faith is something private and personal that we had better keep to ourselves if we want a quiet life. But it really cannot be a matter of indifference to people of faith to see their relatives, friends and neighbours dancing on the broad pagan highway that leads nowhere while all the while they themselves have in their pocket the key to the narrow gate that alone opens onto life.

Faith is meant to be contagious. It reaches out to others and touches them. The Christian vocation is always a missionary vocation. Mission begins at home. We are called to be missionaries within our families. We are called to be missionaries to the next generation as it replaces us. We called to be missionaries to all who share the various little worlds in which we pass our days.

There are, then, questions we all need to face with ourselves. What faith do I actually have? Where did it come from? What am I doing with it? We all need to find our own personal way forward. A first step is to be convinced of that need in an urgent way. The first thing and often the only thing we can do is to take ourselves in hand, confess our sins and do penance. That too is mission beginning at home. We must never let go of the faith that we have professed.

But when we are committed to that, when we are committed to our own ongoing conversion, it is then that little miracles begin to happen, little miracles that confirm us in our faith and enrich the world around us.

Isaiah 53:10-11 / Hebrews 4:14-16 / Mark 10:35-45

Thirtieth Sunday

They go out, they go out full of tears, carrying seed for the sowing: they come back, they come back, full of song, carrying their sheaves.

It is a question, brothers and sisters in Christ, whether or not we can identify with the man at the centre of today's gospel.

He has no name of his own. He is simply BarTimaeus, son of Timaeus. He is blind. He is a beggar. He is sitting at the side of the road. When he shouts out he is scolded and told to keep quiet. As far as the crowd is concerned this is a great moment for them and certainly not the moment for him to be drawing attention to himself. They have always put up with him on condition that he know his place - sitting at the side of the road, at the mercy of their charity. They usually throw him their few spare pennies. It makes them feel better about themselves. If they think about it at all they assume that he must be to blame for his own misfortune. He might even be a fraud. But who cares? God will reward them for their kindness.

Something happens to the man when he grasps that it is Jesus of Nazareth who is the cause of the commotion going on around him. This is no time for playing the usual games and he cries out all his despair: Son of David, have pity on me. And when they scold him and demand that he be quiet he only shouts all the louder: Son of David, have pity on me.

Jesus stops: Call him here. All at once the crowd's attitude changes. Jesus has acknowledged the man. The crowd, taken aback by Jesus' alternative view, force themselves to see him in a new light. Courage, they say, get up; he is calling you. The man knows that this is at last his moment. He throws off his cloak, his cloak that has always been his shelter, his comfort, his protection, even perhaps his disguise. He jumps up and runs recklessly in the direction of Jesus' voice. What do you want me to do for you? What a challenge! What a moment of high drama! What does the man want Jesus to do for him? What will he ask for?

Master, let me see again. Go: your faith has saved you. And immediately his sight returned and he followed Jesus along the road.

Do we have the faith to ask Jesus for what we really need and the courage to follow him along the road?

They go out, they go out full of tears, carrying seed for the sowing: they come back, they come back, full of song, carrying their sheaves.

Jeremiah 31:7-9 / Hebrews 5:1-6 / Mark 10:46-52

Thirty-First Sunday

Listen, Israel: The Lord our God is the one Lord. You shall love the Lord your God with all your heart, with all your soul, with all your strength. Let these words I urge on you this day be written on your heart.

These ancient words, brothers and sister in Christ, are indeed written on the heart of every believing Jew. They are repeated every day as the core of morning and evening prayer and at the approach of death they are repeated quietly a last time.

Listen, Israel: The Lord our God is the one Lord. You shall love the Lord your God with all your heart, with all your soul, with all your strength. These ancient and sacred words are for the faithful Jew the key source of individual identity and social cohesion. You shall repeat them to your children, Moses goes on, and say them over to them whether at rest in your house or walking abroad, at your lying down or at your rising; you shall fasten them on your hand as a sign and on your forehead as a circlet; you shall write them on the doorposts of your house and on your gates.

Those of us who are older remember a time when we Catholics derived a similar confidence in our personal identity and our community belonging from the private piety and public worship of the tradition handed down to us. I remember too as a child being truly impressed at the sight of Belfast Jews, the men and boys sporting their skull caps, as they took the bus to the synagogue on the Sabbath. Nowadays it is our Moslem brothers and sisters who take the prize in our cities for an easy, unselfconscious fidelity to their religious practices.

A medieval parable tells of a sacred ring handed down from father to son which had the effect of making its owner beloved of God and gracious to his fellowmen. It came into the possession of a man who himself had three sons and who, loving all three of them equally, had recklessly promised the ring to each of them.

He had two copies made and on his death bed presented each of the sons with a ring. Naturally they quarrelled when the deception came to light. The wise judge who heard the case put it to them that really it was up to each of them to prove his ring was the genuine one by living a life pleasing to God and beneficial to his fellowmen.

All three of the great religions looking back to Abraham as their father in faith teach that God is one and there is no other. All three of the great religions looking back to Abraham as their father in faith teach that no one truly believes in God until he loves for his brother what he loves for himself.

No one who has grasped this golden rule is far from the kingdom of God, as Jesus himself assures us.

Deuteronomy 6:2-6 / Hebrews 7:23-28 / Mark 12:28-34

Thirty-Second Sunday

When he appears a second time, it will not be to deal with sin but to reward with salvation those who are waiting for him.

We forget, brothers and sisters in Christ, that we are waiting for the Lord to come again. And in that forgetfulness we loose our sense of who we are and what we are about.

If Jesus draws our attention to the generosity of the poor widow captured forever in this splendid gospel page, it is no doubt because it is an image of his own redemptive generosity. Everything has been given. There is nothing left to give. Jesus surrenders himself totally in his death on the cross and in that act of redemptive generosity he opens up for us the way to salvation. If we are to share with him the glory of resurrection we will need, first of all, to share in the sacrificial generosity of his death. Our generosity, our surrender, needs to match his. This is the promise of our Baptism, what we commit ourselves to afresh every time we involve ourselves in the dynamic of the Mass.

Somehow the reality of all this remains strange to us. We have grown comfortable with wrong ideas about God. It is in the silence of the cross that the reality of God comes to meet us, the silence of the cross of Jesus, the mirroring silence of our own cross. We have developed a foolish and superficial way of talking about those many annoyances we identify as our crosses in life. Often it is only afterwards, when we look back, that we can recognize what was, really and truly, our cross at any given time - and we have to admit how awkwardly we carried it and with what bad grace.

Sometimes we were invited to silent acceptance when there was really nothing to be done and instead we lost our peace in an anxious striving to find our own solution. Sometimes we were called to make changes that were needed and instead we lost the initiative in a falsely comforting paralysis. We did not understand that it is a great and special blessing to be able to carry our cross in a fully conscious way.

Almost always indeed, instead of carrying our cross with joy, we refuse to carry it at all - and that is the real tragedy of our lives. A God who asks us to carry our cross with serenity and dignity is too much for us. We are always on the lookout for a nicer God who will free us from our cross and make life easy for us. But, of course, there is no such God.

As we wait for Jesus to appear a second time, let us ask for the grace to imitate his generosity, his total surrender, like the poor widow that day at the Temple treasury, like the poor widow to whom Elijah was sent in time of drought and famine. May we come to recognise our own cross, accept it with joy and carry it with dignity into the glory of heaven.

First Kings 17:10-16 / Hebrews 9:24-28 / Mark 12:38-44

Thirty-Third Sunday

When that time comes, your own people will be spared, all those whose names are found written in the Book.

On this last Sunday but one of the Church year, brothers and sisters in Christ, our tradition invites us to ponder the four last things. They are called the last things because they are what will come at the end: Death, Judgment, Heaven, Hell. And, of course, the term is not inappropriate for another reason: these are often the very last things that any of us think about as we follow our daily round.

Yet perhaps the most striking difference between us and other creatures is that we are to some extent aware that death awaits us. In fact our attitude to our own death determines in great measure how we live our lives. We are challenged to make sense of who we are even though we know that a day will come when the world will get on perfectly well without us. Death is more than an appalling thing that happens to other people. Death is more than a tragedy that deprives us of those we love. Death is an unavoidable moment in our own personal destiny and we know neither the day nor the hour. Death is our own personal apocalyptic moment, even though we may well live long enough to greet the ancient enemy as a friend. Death is, quite literally, the end of the world for us. For indeed every death is the end of a world. A light goes out and the final sentence of every biography is written in the dark.

What happens next? The Christian tradition speaks of a moment of judgment in which we become who we are once and for all. In death we are thrust out into God. Some find themselves at home with God. That is where they belong - in heaven. Others are not yet ready for God and they experience the purification that we call purgatory. Others still find that they do not belong with God at all but they have nowhere else to go and so they are stuck - as stuck in death as they were in life. Yes, that much at least no one will want to dispute: You don't have to wait for death to experience hell. Hell is the reality of a great many people's lives here and now: cut off from God, cut off from their true selves, cut off from those around them in the isolation of compulsion and fantasy.

The message of Jesus is that we don't have to sit life out waiting for death and judgment. Today is the day of salvation. Today is the first day of the rest of our lives. If we were to embark upon our purgatory today we could get it out of the way and spend years in heaven before death overtakes us at all. The invitation is to enter into a different kind of dying, the promise of our baptism that if we die with Christ we shall also live with him. We are invited to die to sin and selfishness. It is a painful death, this crucifixion of our false self - but it is the price of life. If we have died with him we shall surely live with him. Already now today and for all eternity.

Daniel 12:1-13 / Hebrews 10:11-14. 18 /
Mark 13:24-32

Printed in Great Britain
by Amazon